WOW DAD!

**71 ways to be
the wonderful, fun, smart parent
you always knew you were**

Peter Atkinson

Best Guess Publishing
#238, 1919B – 4 Street s.w.
Calgary, Alberta T2S 1W4 Canada

Phone: (403) 244•8688
Fax: (403) 244•8670

E-mail: inquiries@wowdad.com
Web: www.wowdad.com

CANADIAN CATALOGUING IN PUBLICATION DATA

Atkinson, Peter, 1961 –
Wow Dad !

Includes index
ISBN: 0-9685129-0-9

1. Family recreation. 2. Games. I Title.
GV182.8.A84 1999   790.1'91   C99-910567-1
Printed in Canada

Credits: Editorial: Sheila Bean
Illustrations: original drawings of the human form, by Anjan Raymond-Bhatt; other diagrams by Jeremy Drought
Cover and Interior Design: Jeremy Drought
Production: Last Impression Publishing Service, Calgary, Alberta
Back Cover Photo: William Atkinson
Printing: Friesens, Altona, Manitoba

DEDICATION

This book, like everything else I do, is for my son, Scott.

To: Jeff (DAD)

FROM: Dad (GRANDDAD)

Son, I know that you will be the bestest Dad
love, Dad.

iii

ACKNOWLEDGMENTS

One of the best things about publishing a book is that you get to thank people in writing for helping you do something that you love doing. Somehow putting it in print makes it seem extra-special. Like these people.

First I have to thank my friend Garth, who never stopped asking me when the book was coming out. And I mean never. OK, G., you can stop now.

Jeremy Drought, who designed the book you're now holding, was instrumental in getting this done. Jeremy braved all the hand-wringing and dumb questions of someone new to the publishing business (me) and never allowed me to go off on some of my stranger tangents (although I still think that the 'scratch 'n' sniff' chapter is a great idea). He also helped with a lot of the business side of publishing books, strange mystical things I had no idea about and without which I would probably be in jail now.

This is fun. Who else can I thank? Well, my son, Scott, for innocently being the guinea pig for so much of the book's content. Jenny for her steady faith, her patient understanding, and her calm support. My parents for, well, all the stuff that I wish Scott was thanking me for now: changing my diapers, making my lunch for school, buying me clothes over the years instead of buying themselves a Caribbean cruise, etc., etc., etc.

And last, but not least, I thank you, the person reading this. And the person reading it over your shoulder. Thanks for getting my book.

Peter Atkinson

FOREWORD

Walk through any major bookstore, in any city in Canada or the United States, and you will find a section devoted to parenting books.

Unfortunately, for fathers seeking parenting assistance, information on child development, or just ideas on how to have fun with the kids, a leisurely stroll through the bookstore is unlikely to yield anything that will grab their attention. Whether you scan the book titles or look at the pictures on the book covers, you could be excused for thinking "These books are for mothers" or "I guess only mothers want to spend time with their children" or "Where's daddy?" If you actually open these books and read them, it will become clear that mothers and fathers don't need different rules or ideas for being parents—but few fathers will get that far, because most parenting books are not marketed with them in mind.

Into this void comes Peter Atkinson's *WOW DAD!* books. The title will get fathers' attention—but mothers, don't be put off, for there are wonderful ideas for both mothers and fathers in the books. Whether your goal is to make bathtime more fun or to introduce your youngsters to the magic of nature, there are suggestions here that you can use. Try some, and learn from your children what they like and don't like. More important, use them just to spend time talking, joking, and playing with your kids, for that is the real joy of being a parent.

John Hunsley, Ph.D., C.Psych.
Professor, School of Psychology, and Director, Centre for Psychological Services
University of Ottawa
Ottawa, March 1999

TABLE OF CONTENTS

Table of Contents

Table of Contents

WOW DAD!

INTRODUCTION

When my son, Scott, was about three years old, I noticed how much he enjoyed the little things that I did for him: flipping a coin, flying a paper airplane, skipping a rock. A trip to the fair was a great way to spend a couple of hours with him, but so was throwing rocks into a stream.

As a first-time father, I was putting a lot of time and energy into 'wowing' Scott. But he didn't need it. I talked to other parents, teachers, and eventually child psychologists, and everyone agreed that the most important thing for children was to have both parents happily involved in their lives.

I learned that a lot of parents are good at creating special events, but have forgotten the importance of special moments. And it's these moments that children treasure and remember, and that create real bonds between each parent and child.

Sometimes a big event is just plain wonderful. Every child should be taken to the circus when it's in town. But as we get caught up in our busy lives, maybe the event becomes a way to compensate for working late and not being around as much as we want. And, sadly, there are some parents who don't know what else to do with their children or even how to communicate with them.

It seemed to me that with all the 25-screen theatres and 3-D video games out there, we might forget how easy it is to do something special for a child. So I started making a list of the little tricks and fun things that had created so many special moments for Scott and me. I remembered games that my father had shown me, I did some reading, some of my friends added their own ideas, and before I knew it, I had enough to share here.

WOW DAD!

With the tips in these books, anyone can create fun and memories with children anywhere and anytime. The activities are fun, fast, simple to prepare, and easy to do. You may find that some of them stimulate a few questions along the way, and the search for the answers will create more special moments for you.

I get a thrill when Scott looks at me like I'm the greatest thing since the Muppets. Cultivating curiosity in a child is definitely a worthy goal. But the real fun of these books is to make your child say "Wow Dad!" because after "I love you," that is the greatest sound of all.

Peter Atkinson
Calgary, March 1999

BEFORE YOU START

We are participants in the lives of our children. We ask questions and encourage answers. But wouldn't it be nice if we could be the show every now and then?

Take a moment to look through this book in private. Decide which of the tricks you like and maybe even practise them once or twice to make sure you know how to do them. This is not dishonest. This is smart. It doesn't matter whether you learned to do these things 20 years ago or 20 minutes ago, as long as you share them with your children.

Learn a few at a time and whip them out whenever you can. Some tricks and activities are a solo performance, but many are shared games you and even your very young children can play together.

For this reason, a 'Suitable for Ages...' guide has intentionally been left out. Younger children will usually be happy just to watch you perform, while older ones might want to know how a trick works. Beyond pure fun, these things evoke a rich and exciting wealth of ideas and images that integrate listening, observing, and thinking skills.

And that leads to a small caution as well.

Pay attention to your audience. Any child will quickly turn off something that's frightening or frustrating. So don't get so caught up in your performance that you fail to notice if your audience is enjoying it or not. If your child is too young for something, you can always come back to it in a year or two. If your child is too old for it, move on to the next activity. Remember that your main goal is to spend quality time with your child.

WOW DAD!

Don't forget that what might not amaze you will amaze your child. Something that you've known for 20 or 30 years is brand-new to a youngster. You can introduce a trick and in the process connect with the thrill and excitement of your child's discovery.

One final note. There is no sexism in this book. Some tips refer to the child as him, and some as her. I have tried to use both terms equally.

Now, go out there and show your child that you are the most magical and wonderful person in the world.

Have fun!

THE GREAT OUTDOORS

THE WONDERS OF THE NIGHT SKY

Although city lights drown out most of the stars in the night sky, the stars you'll be looking for here are bright enough to be seen from just about anywhere. But no childhood should be without a trip to the country to soak up all the stars the eye can see.

FIRST, FIND THE NORTH STAR

The North Star, also known as *Polaris*, is part of the Little Dipper constellation, which can be found in relation to the more obvious Big Dipper.

The constellations change their position in the sky as the Earth moves around the Sun but their shape and their angle to each other remains the same. Because of this you can always use the Big Dipper to find the Little Dipper and then the North Star.

To find the North Star, just focus on the Big Dipper's bowl and the two stars forming it that are the farthest from the handle. If you follow a line from these stars, above the open bowl of the Dipper, you will come to the North Star, which sits at the tip of the handle of the Little Dipper.

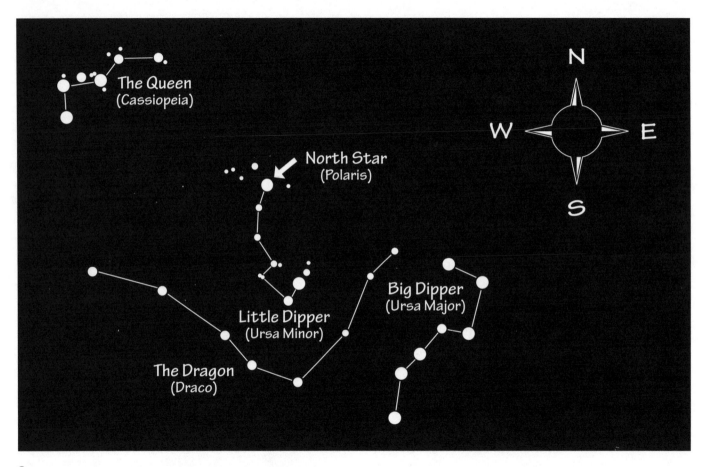

The Little Dipper is actually part of a constellation called *Ursa Minor*, The Little Bear. (Yes, the Big Dipper is also called *Ursa Major*, The Big Bear.) These constellations are a good starting point to find two other constellations that can be seen year-round.

The third year-round constellation is *Cassiopeia*, the Queen. It looks like the letter M in winter or a W in summer. To find her, look from the middle star in the Big Dipper's handle through the North Star. This line will carry your eye to *Cassiopeia*.

The other year-round constellation is *Draco*, the Dragon. To find *Draco*, just move your eyes out from the bowl of the Big Dipper, as if it were going to scoop up the next stars above it. That's *Draco's* tail. Or its head, depending on how you look at it. Anyway, you've found it.

All of these constellations include fairly bright stars and are easy to recognize, even for young children.

There are lots of other easy-to-spot constellations that appear at different times of the year, so if your child enjoys this, keep going. The sky really is the limit!

REMEMBERING THE ORDER OF THE PLANETS

While we're speaking of the sky, here's a simple way to remember the order of the planets. In order moving away from the Sun, they are: Mercury, Venus, Earth, Mars, Jupiter, Saturn, Uranus, Neptune, and Pluto.

But it's not the names that are so hard to remember, it's the order. So try passing on this memory trick:

My Very Educated Mother Just Served Us Nine Pizzas

There you have it. Much easier, isn't it?

WHISTLING GRASS

Whistling is too kind a word to describe this sound. Screaming is more like it. I've decided that it's too difficult to explain in words, so just follow the illustrations. The only trick is to use the ring finger of one hand to hold the bottom of the blade of grass in place until the base of the thumb on your other hand takes over. See what I mean? Just trust me, it's all in the pictures.

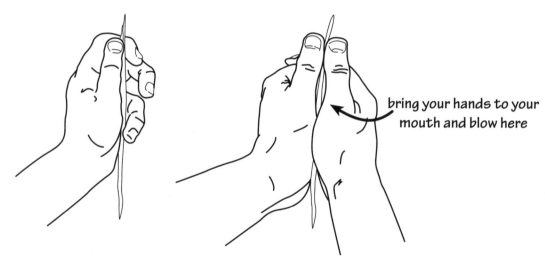

bring your hands to your mouth and blow here

grass in left fingers, lying on base of thumb, and ring finger of left hand comes down to hold bottom of grass

base of right thumb squeezes bottom of the grass while the top of the right thumb squeezes top of grass

DANDELION CHAINS

This is an old favourite that turns a bunch of weeds into a wonderful pastime. Start by finding a field of dandelions and getting yourselves comfortable right in the thick of it. And just start picking.

Make sure you pick the dandelions down low, close to the bottom of the stem. Then use your thumbnail or fingernail to make a small slit in the stem, just long enough to pass the next dandelion stem through. (For very young children, you can divide the labour, with you being the splitter and your child doing the actual stringing together.)

You can make victory wreaths à la ancient Rome, necklaces, bracelets, and chains as long as you want. They make great gifts and very special souvenirs.

ROCK SKIPPING

A good rock skipper can skip just about any rock, but the ideal skipping rock has at least one flat side with a nice rounded shape that fits well into the first finger and thumb of your throwing hand.

Fortunately, especially for beginners, it's amazing just how many of these there are around. The key to a successful throw is to get down low. Bring the foot opposite your throwing hand a step forward, bend your knees, and lean to the same side as your throwing hand. Then use a side-arm motion to throw the rock across the surface of the water.

Once you get the motion down, it becomes pretty easy. Soon you'll be able to skip almost any rock at least a couple of bounces. Good skipping rocks, and good rock skippers, will often get 10 or more bounces from a single rock.

Now, there's something to aim for!

THE PERFECT SANDCASTLE

Whether you're building a miniature sandcastle or a monstrous sand dragon, the secret to good sand is...water.

The sand is constantly drying out while you're building, so the trick is to keep your sculpture's sand wet. Professional sand sculptors (yes, there are such lucky people) use little spray bottles to do this, but gently splashing from a bucket of water will work just as well.

The closer you build to the water's edge, the wetter the sand (and the shorter the trip when carrying buckets of water to your construction site). Find a site where the sand is wet enough to start building without any added water— but not so close to the water that the tide will wash away your work.

Of course, if your sand is *too* wet, then it will just ooze away. With a little practice you'll learn to recognize when the sand needs wetting and when it has hardened enough for any shaping you might want to do. If something does crumble away, it can be rebuilt by moistening what's left and adding more wet sand.

Keep in mind that a sandcastle doesn't have to be made of just sand, and that you can build something other than a castle. You can use toys or anything else (such as twigs, seaweed, and leaves) that's lying around to decorate your construction to fit the fantasies of your child.

TAKE SOME TIME

Try this while you're out sitting in the dandelions—or anywhere else outdoors, for that matter.

Lie down on the grass with your child to watch the drifting clouds. You can trade ideas about the smell of the grass, the feel of the wind, and the sound of any birds or bugs chirping away nearby. And you can both relax. Even the most active child will appreciate the time to look and listen.

If you're feeling energetic, you can look for familiar shapes in the clouds. This is good for everyone's imagination, so let yours soar, too. There could be boats, animals, dinosaurs, people, and more floating by up there. Remember, there are no wrong answers.

It's also a good time just to talk. See what comes up.

FUN IN THE DARK

HAND SHADOWS

Remember hand shadows? You can do these with just about any kind of light on any kind of flat surface, whether it's a flashlight on a tent or a lamp on a bedroom wall. Experiment to find the best distance between the light and your hands to get the clearest shadows possible.

One of the best places to do this is at night just before bed. It can be an especially fun way to help a child who is afraid when the lights go out.

You can build a good repertoire of these but the most fun will come from trying to invent your own. Here are some to get you started:

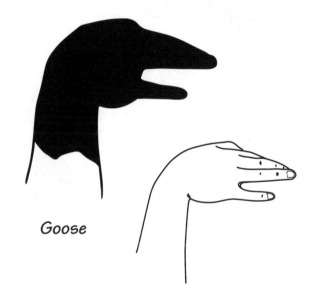

Goose

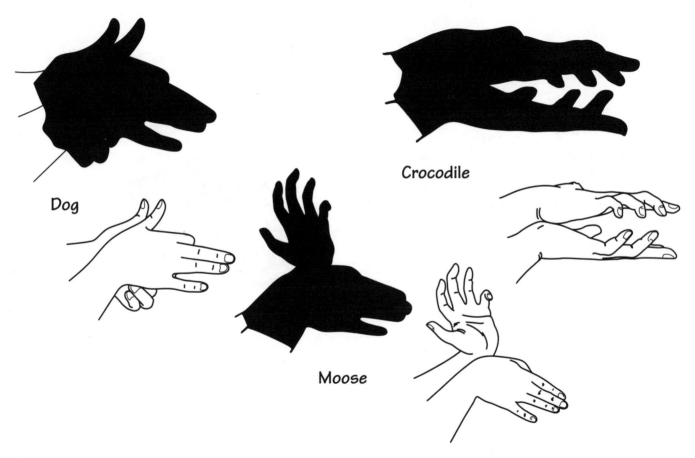

Dog

Crocodile

Moose

FLASHLIGHT FUN

Before bedtime, you can also do some exploring when the lights are out. Take a flashlight and explore your home together in the dark. You'll be surprised how different things look, and what you'll see that you never noticed before.

Another fun-in-the-dark game is flashlight-hide-and-seek. (This is only recommended for children who are past their lights-out fears.) As usual, the hiders hide but the seeker has to spot them with a beam of light from the flashlight.

You can make this more challenging by playing without the flashlight. This turns even a so-so hiding place into a great one as long as the hiders can keep quiet!

A Safety Note: Don't try these games in complete darkness. Better to leave a light on somewhere than to have to cancel the game due to injuries.

PAPER AIRPLANES

Throwing things made from paper is fun anytime. It's especially good for a rainy day indoors because unless your child throws like Nolan Ryan there are very, very few things that paper can break.

Let's start with the basics. Most of us have made this simple paper airplane before, but just in case the memory is a little hazy, here it is again.

THE ORIGINAL DART

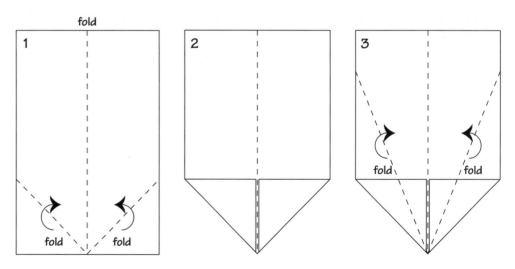

THE ORIGINAL DART – continued:

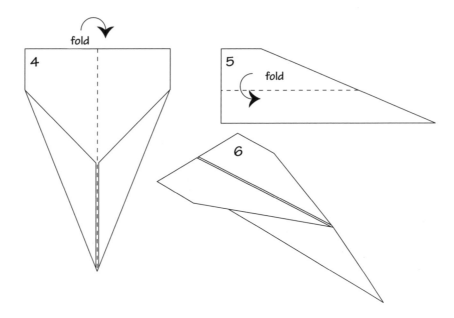

THE BULLET

The next step up is this hot little number:

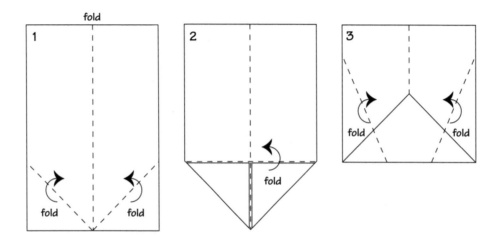

THE BULLET – continued:

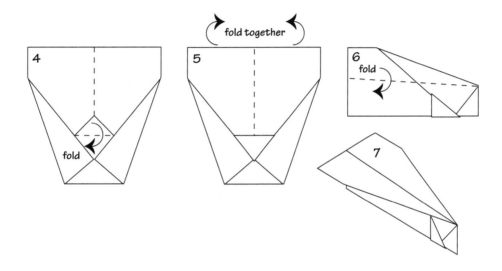

THE SPINNER

And who said flight had to be straight? This one is made to dip and curve:

Start by creating a square of paper:

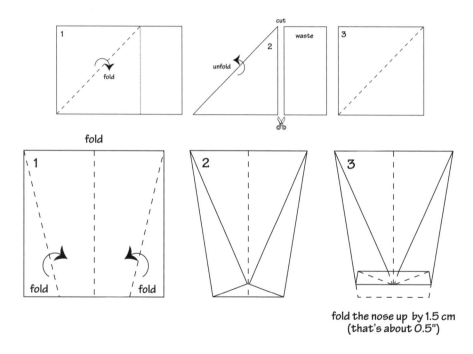

fold the nose up by 1.5 cm
(that's about 0.5")

THE SPINNER – continued:

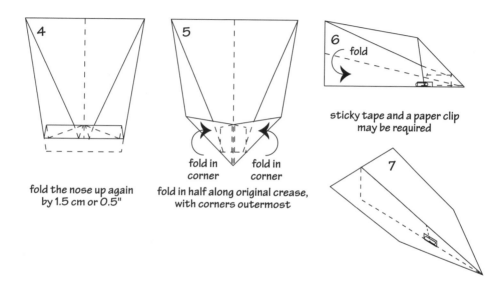

4

fold the nose up again
by 1.5 cm or 0.5"

5

fold in
corner

fold in
corner

fold in half along original crease,
with corners outermost

6 fold

sticky tape and a paper clip
may be required

7

THE CHOPPER

Here's how to make a helicopter, to complete your air force:

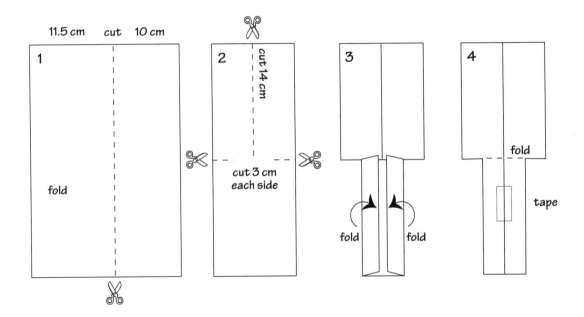

THE CHOPPER – continued:

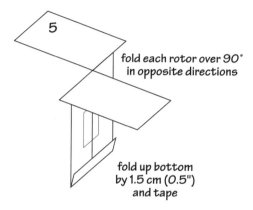

5

fold each rotor over 90°
in opposite directions

fold up bottom
by 1.5 cm (0.5")
and tape

AIRPLANE MARKINGS

You can add to the fun by drawing shapes and colors on your airplanes to create a whole air force of fun flyers. Here are just a few suggestions: a globe, a hammer and sickle, a maple leaf, a Canada goose, a fleur-de-lys, and a five-point star.

WATER TRICKS

BATHTIME SCIENCE

Follow these directions for some fun in the bath. (I don't have to remind you to use a glass made of plastic and not glass, just in case of accidents, do I?)

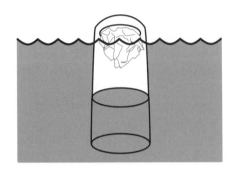

Push a dry cloth or a piece of tissue to the bottom of a tall glass and put the glass in the water with the open end facing down. Ask your child to look inside and he will see that the glass is still partly empty. When you lift the glass out of the water, the cloth will still be dry!

This happens because of air pressure: as the glass is pushed into the water, the air in the glass has nowhere to go and gets squeezed against the bottom. There's no more room in the glass for the water, and so the cloth stays dry.

Next, remove the cloth, put the glass under the surface of the bath, and let it fill with water. Keep the glass underwater and turn it upside-down so that the open end faces down. Now slowly raise the glass. If you keep the rim below the surface of the bath water, the water in the glass won't spill out, thanks once again to air pressure. This time, because there's no way for the air to get inside, there's nothing to force the water out.

WATER SQUIRTING

This is a simple trick and one that is gentle enough to do with even very young children.

Make the first two fingers and the thumb of your hand into a loose fist with the first finger just at or above the surface of the water. Now, bring the other two fingers in quickly towards your palm and water will squirt out. Not very far and not very high but enough to surprise and get a few laughs.

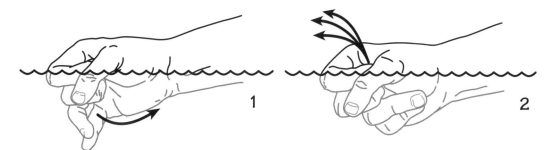

BUBBLES, BUBBLES EVERYWHERE

MAKE YOUR OWN BUBBLE MIX

While there is nothing wrong with most commercial bubble solutions, some of us are just determined to do everything ourselves. Here's the formula for a good homemade brew:

In 1 cup (250 ml) of water, combine 1 cup (250 ml) of liquid detergent and (the secret ingredient) 1 cup (250 ml) of glycerine, which you can buy from your local drugstore. You might play around with a little more glycerine to make more durable bubbles, but that's it.

BUBBLE SHAPES

You can make bubbles with different shapes. Just take a wire coat hanger, bend it into the shape you want, and dip it into your bubble mix. With something this size, rather than blow through it, you gently swing the frame through the air to make the bubbles flow.

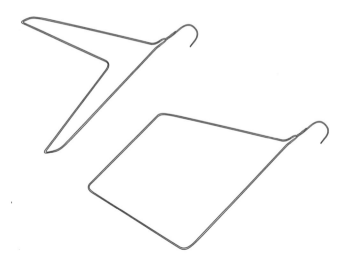

If you want to play with your bubble shapes, you can make a flexible frame by running a piece of string through two straws, as shown opposite:

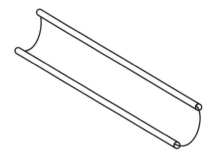

Once your shape is ready, fill a flat baking pan or a bowl big enough to immerse the frame in the bubble solution. Dip the frame into it. The solution will fill the frame with a flat bubble that can be twisted and turned. (Try gently pushing things through the bubble and see what happens.) To make a round bubble, just bring the straws together so that they touch.

Another easy-to-find and easy-to-use bubble frame is the ringed plastic that holds together six-packs of canned drinks. It will give you lots of bubbles at once.

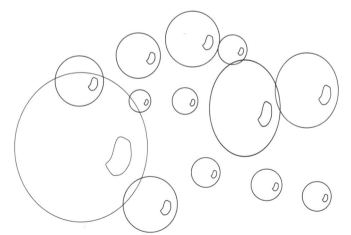

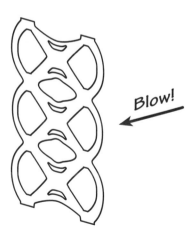

Blow!

DISHTIME FUN

You can even make bubbles while doing the dishes together.

Pour some water into a glass or a bowl. Put a drop or two of dish soap on the surface of the water but don't mix it in. Touch a finger to these soap drops and then touch the hole in the soap-bottle cap. This puts a soapy film over the hole so that when you or your child squeezes the bottle, the air that's forced out makes bubbles.

This works best if the bottle is at least one-third empty so that there is enough air inside to push out. Try squeezing quickly and slowly to create bubbles of different sizes.

BUBBLE VOLCANO

To make some seriously out-of-control bubbles, try this bubble mixture:

Combine two big spoonfuls of vinegar and a spoonful of liquid soap in a half-full glass of water. Then add one big spoonful of baking soda and stand back! The baking soda and vinegar react in the water to give off a gas, which turns the soap into bubbles with a very visible, and fun, result.

Hint: This can get messy so try it outside or at least in the sink or bathtub.

THINKING OUTSIDE THE LINES

I like these next few because you have to think a little differently to find the answers. Sometimes a change of perspective does us all good.

Try to solve them yourself before you go to the answers on the next page.

Draw a third arrow with only two lines:

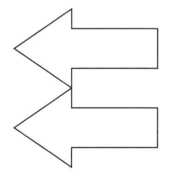

Connect all the dots with just four straight lines:

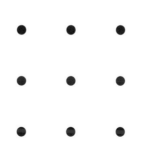

Solve this riddle:

A woman leaves her house and walks 500 miles north, 500 miles west, and 500 miles south to arrive back home. When she gets there she sees a bear. *What colour is the bear?*

Can you solve these before you peek at the answers on the next page?

WOW DAD!

See, with just two lines, you can make a third arrow!

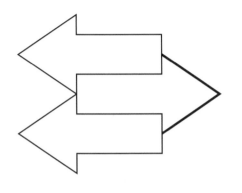

See, four lines can join all the dots, when you think outside the box!

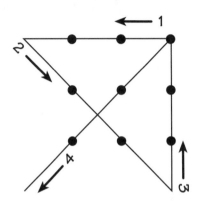

The answer to the riddle is:

I bet you didn't expect the question about the bear. Well, the answer is white, and here's why: to arrive home on that route, the walker's 500 miles west has to circle the globe, and the only place where the world is narrow enough for this itinerary is at the top. So the woman is somewhere in the Arctic and the bear is a polar bear. Sure, it's a little far-fetched but, hey, it's a riddle.

TONGUE TWISTERS

Children love hearing silly sounds and rhymes, so try saying each of these three times fast for fun. If you get them right, you get silly rhymes, if you get them wrong, you get silly sounds. You can't lose!

There's the old standby:

Peter Piper picked a peck of pickled peppers. If Peter Piper picked a peck of pickled peppers, how many pickled peppers did Peter Piper pick?

And these trickier ones:

Which thrush whistles?

The sixth sheik's sixth sheep is sick.

She sells seashells by the seashore.

I want coffee in a proper copper coffee pot.

Round and round the ragged rock the ragged rascal ran.

You can ask the tongue-twisting question:

How much wood would a woodchuck chuck if a woodchuck could chuck wood?

And you can answer with:

A woodchuck would chuck all the wood he could chuck if a woodchuck could chuck wood.

And along the same lines:

How much ground would a groundhog grind if a groundhog could grind ground?

A groundhog would grind all the ground he could grind if a groundhog could grind ground.

FUN IN A RESTAURANT

Sitting and waiting for food with hungry children shouldn't be torture. Play around with some of these, and your food will arrive before you know it.

SPOON BALANCING

You too can balance a spoon on your nose! The trick is to breathe gently on the bowl of the spoon where you would normally put your food. The moisture from your breath helps stop the spoon from slipping off your nose. All you have to worry about is finding just the right place on your nose to hang the spoon.

MUSICAL GLASSES

If you're at the kind of restaurant where they serve water in real glass, gather everyone's water glasses in front of you and either drink, or have them drunk from, so that each one contains a different level of water.

Moisten the tip of your finger, rub it around the rim of each glass, and listen. You'll be making music. Let everyone have a try and you can be a (quiet) table band!

FUN WITH A STRAW

Yes, it's true. There is a trick you can do with a straw and not much else.

It involves creating a vacuum in a straw, which can be handy for...well, not for much, except that it's fun to see.

First, stick the straw into your drink. Then either cover the top of the straw with your finger or thumb, or pinch the hole shut. When you lift the straw out of the glass, as long as you keep the top hole closed, nothing will come out.

But be warned that as soon as you remove your finger, whatever's inside the straw will spill out, so be careful where you have it when you let go!

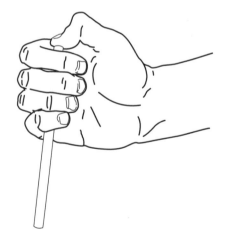

TABLE SOCCER

If you're in the right kind of restaurant, you might want to try a game of table soccer.

All you need are two straws, a crumpled piece of paper for a ball, and some lungpower. You move the 'ball' by blowing through your straw. Every time you blow the 'ball' off your opponent's edge of the table it's a goal.

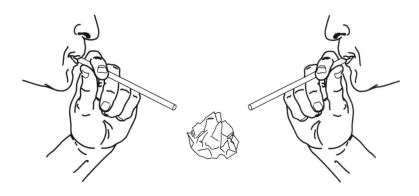

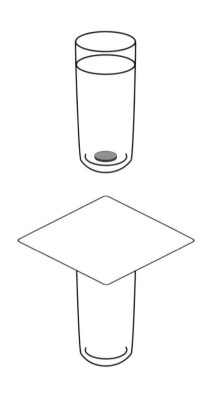

TABLE MAGIC

You might also want to pass the time by making something disappear.

Take a glass with a thin bottom and set it on top of something flat and easily seen through the water, such as a piece of coloured paper or a coin (a penny works well because of its dark colour).

Now put a piece of paper or a plate on the rim so that you can't look straight down through the water. When your child looks through the side to see the object underneath, it will have disappeared! But when you lift off the cover and look down, it's still there!

Light bends as it passes through water, so the image of the penny can't be seen from the side.

PENNY CLEANER

Before you make the penny disappear, you might want to clean it first.

All you have to do is lay the penny on a plate and cover it thoroughly with a sprinkling of salt. Add a few drops of vinegar to the salt pile, wait a bit, and you will have one very clean penny!

SUPER PAPER

Did you know that a piece of paper can hold up a glass of water?

There's a trick to it, of course, and the trick to this trick is to fold the paper accordion-style to strengthen it. Balance the paper across two more glasses, with the folds running lengthwise between the glasses. Stand the glass of water on top of the paper and you've done it!

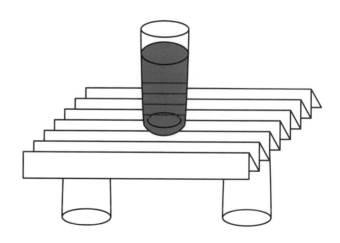

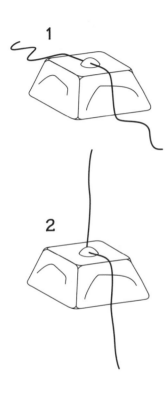

ICE HOLDER

Here's a very interesting trick that takes a minute to do but is worth the wait.

Lay a piece of thread across an ice cube. Sprinkle some salt over the cube, making sure you hit the part with the string on it. Wait a minute, then take hold of the string and lift. Amazingly, the ice cube will come up with it.

Just as salt melts snow on a sidewalk, the salt melts a little bit of the ice cube, creating a mini-puddle. The rest of the ice cube is still cold, so after a minute or so the puddle freezes again, with the thread attached.

A TASTELESS TRICK

Once your food does arrive, you can still have a little more fun. Ask your child to plug his nose as he takes a bite. He won't be able to taste his food.

The sense of smell and the sense of taste are closely connected. And so can be the sense of fun.

NUMBER STUMPERS

You know that if you're making mathematics fun, you must be really smart. These simple math games just might do the trick.

You could use a calculator for some of these but you might also get older children to do the calculations themselves; often once they see the answers they want to work out the pattern to see how it happened. "What?" you say. "A child doing math voluntarily?" It can happen.

These problems all use basic arithmetic, nothing fancier than division, but you should make sure your child is old enough to understand the idea of the bigger numbers you get in some cases.

These first few make repeating sequences of numbers:

$$0 \times 9 + 1 = 1$$

$$1 \times 9 + 2 = 11$$

$$12 \times 9 + 3 = 111$$

$$123 \times 9 + 4 = 1,111$$

$$1234 \times 9 + 5 = 11,111 \quad \text{... etc.}$$

And these:

$$143 \times 2 \times 7 = 2,002$$

$$143 \times 3 \times 7 = 3,003$$

$$143 \times 4 \times 7 = 4,004$$

$$143 \times 5 \times 7 = 5,005 \quad \text{... etc.}$$

WOW DAD!

And another one:

Take any single-digit number. Multiply it by 9 and then by 12345679. (Make sure that you don't insert an 8 into that big number.) For example:

$$3 \times 9 \times 12345679 = 33,333,333$$

$$2 \times 9 \times 12345679 = 22,222,222$$

These next ones are number formulas you can do together. It makes you look smart and math look fun. Not bad!

For this next one you pick the number 8 and your child picks a random, single-digit number (e.g., 5).

Double your child's number	$(2 \times 5 = 10)$
Add 2	$(10 + 2 = 12)$
Multiply by 5	$(12 \times 5 = 60)$
Subtract 2	$(60 - 2 = 58)$

The first digit is the one your child picked; the second one is yours.

And maybe just one more:

Take any number between 1 and 9, add 3, multiply by 2, subtract 2, divide by 2, subtract 2 again, and you get the original number.

For example, using 5:

$5 + 3 = 8, \times 2 = 16, - 2 = 14, \div 2 = 7, - 2 = 5$

And using 8:

$8 + 3 = 11, \times 2 = 22, - 2 = 20, \div 2 = 10, - 2 = 8$

ROPE TRICKS

ALL THE KNOTS YOU'LL NEED

There are basically three kinds of tying that you'll ever do: a rope to something else (hitches), a rope to another rope (bends), and a rope into a loop. Here are three simple knots, one for each of these situations. Just follow the illustrations and you can't go wrong.

CLOVE HITCH: a rope-to-something-else knot

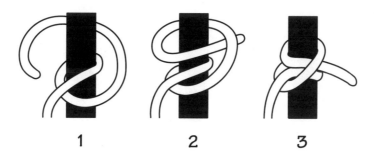

1   2   3

WOW DAD!

SHEET BEND: a rope-to-a-rope knot

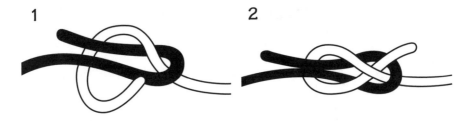

1

2

BOWLINE: a loop knot

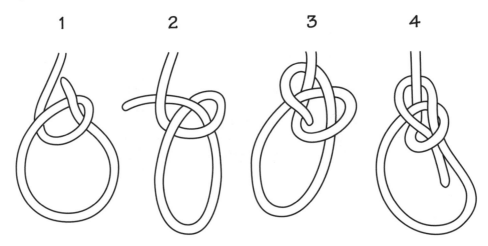

1   2   3   4

THE TRANSFER OF CURVES

This is based on a scientific principle called the *Transfer of Curves*, which is kind of fun—especially for a scientific principle.

Lay a piece of string on a table and announce that you will tie a knot by touching only the ends of the string and without letting go of it. Now cross your arms in front of you. With your arms still crossed, pick up an end of the string in each hand and hold it as you uncross your arms. You will make an instant knot as the curves transfer from your arms to the string.

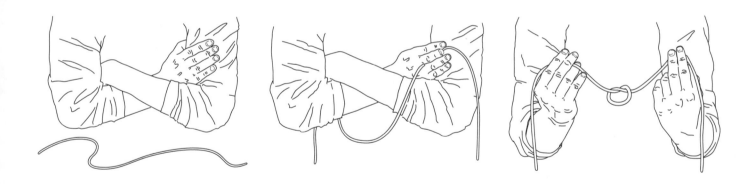

THE ROPE THAT TIES ITSELF

This one might take some practice but the effect is worth it.

Use a heavy piece of rope, about a metre long, with a knot at one end. Let it hang from your hand, with the knot at the bottom. Start by flipping the knotted end up over your arm.

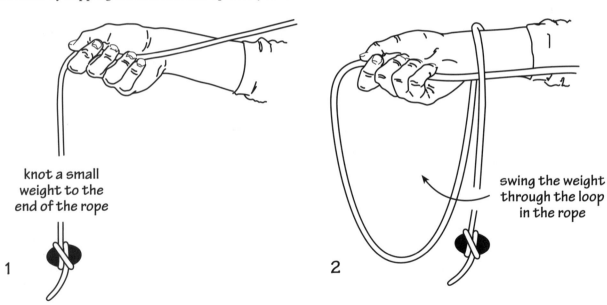

knot a small
weight to the
end of the rope

1

swing the weight
through the loop
in the rope

2

Move your arm gently to swing the knotted end through the loop you've just made and then quickly pull your hand back towards you. Voila! Instant knot.

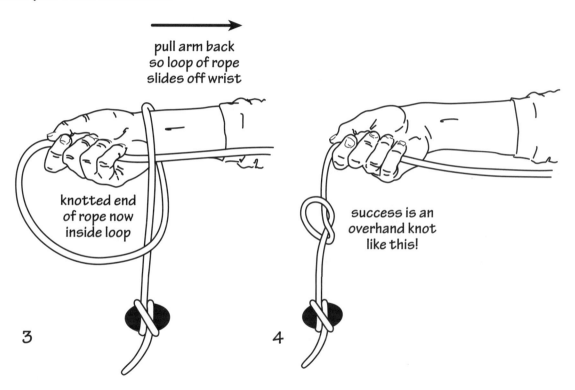

pull arm back
so loop of rope
slides off wrist

knotted end
of rope now
inside loop

success is an
overhand knot
like this!

3

4

HOMEMADE TATTOOS

First, choose a design for your tattoo, keeping it simple to start with. Draw the picture on paper with a normal soft-lead pencil, going over the design several times so that the lines are nice and dark. Now thoroughly moisten the skin where the tattoo will be applied. Press the paper firmly on the body part of the tattooee and rub gently. Peel the paper off and you will have a homemade tattoo.

For something just a little more permanent, you can draw your design in pen right on your child's skin and colour it in with felt markers. (The water-soluble kind will be easier to wash off when you're ready for a change.)

COIN GAMES

Good for rainy days or for dry ones, all you need to play these very portable games are a flat table and some coins. Add a little imagination and you have a major sporting event.

A quarter works best for the football and basketball games, while nickels or pennies are the best size for bowling, hockey, and soccer.

These games are also very fair. This is because the size of the goal or net you are shooting at depends on the size of the hands forming them and your (probably) superior coordination will be offset by your child's smaller hands!

There are two techniques for moving the coins, either with the side of the finger or with the fingernails, as shown right:

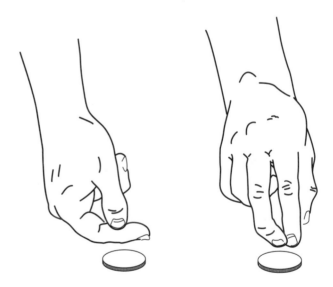

WOW DAD!

Two general rules apply to all of the games:

If a coin falls off the table at any time, it's the other player's turn.

It's usually better to play across the width of the table and not its length. This is so that everyone can reach and because it makes for a faster game.

Other than that, don't worry about changing the rules of the games if you want. The only rule you can't change is that you have to have fun.

FOOTBALL

To start the game, the defending player 'kicks off' by placing a coin at the edge of the table and pushing it as deep as possible into the other team's half, that is, as close to the opposite edge of the table without having it fall off. (If the coin does fall off, the receiving team starts by placing the coin one hand's length from the edge.)

The receiving team then has four chances to move the coin back downfield (or downtable) into scoring position.

Scoring position means that part of the coin is hanging over the edge of the table. The defence then has a chance to make a goal line stand by using a finger to flip the coin into the air and catch it. If the coin is caught, then no score.

(**IMPORTANT**: The last move with the coin can be a move backwards, making less of the coin hang over. The more of the coin that hangs over the table, the easier it is to get a good, high flick, making it easier to catch. You can use this knowledge as you see fit, possibly to keep the game close, if you know what I mean.)

 hard easy

If the coin isn't in a position to be flipped after four downs, the other player takes over possession and has his turn to score.

Once a touchdown is scored, the offence goes for an extra point by spinning the coin on the table, trying to catch it between his thumbs, and flicking the coin through the goal posts made by the other player's two hands. (You can skip this part if your child is too young or is having trouble spinning the coin.)

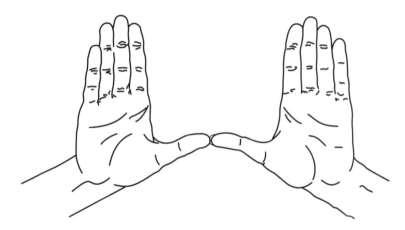

Just like the real thing, play restarts with another kickoff.

BASKETBALL

This game simply takes the field-goal technique of coin football and makes it into a whole game.

Start by spinning a quarter and trying to catch it between your two thumbs before it stops spinning. The offence may blow on the spinning quarter to help move it to the best shooting position. (You can allow the defence to blow, too, if you want to make this more difficult!)

Once you catch the coin you can shoot for the basket. This is the basket:

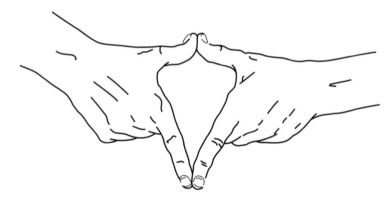

If the coin isn't caught before it stops spinning or if it spins off the table, your opponent takes possession.

HOCKEY

The game begins with the offence dropping three coins on the table. To move for a shot on net, you shoot any coin between the other two. If the moving coin hits either of the other coins, or if it goes less than half its diameter through them, the other player takes over. There's no limit to the number of shots a player can take.

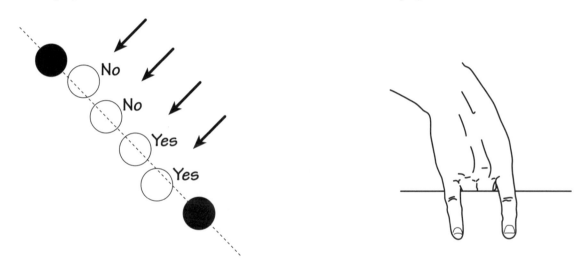

A goal is scored by shooting on a goal made by the first and last fingers of the opposition's hand.

Remember that a shot on net still has to pass between the two other coins.

SOCCER

This game is played like hockey but it becomes a little more involved because each player gets to set up a defence and a goalkeeper. These can be placed anywhere along the imaginary lines as shown below. Once set up, the defence coins don't move unless they are hit by one of the other coins. If this does happen, the attacking team loses possession and the 'defender' is put back into position.

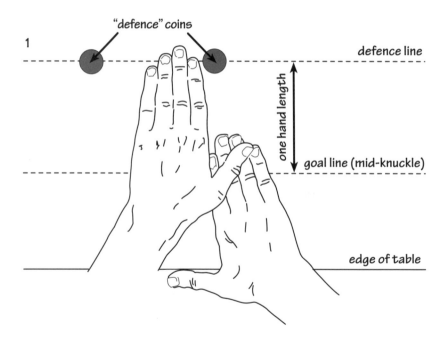

If the goalkeeper coin is hit by another coin, then no goal is scored. As you improve at this game, you can make it more difficult to score by allowing the defence to move the goalkeeper coin along the goal line before a shot.

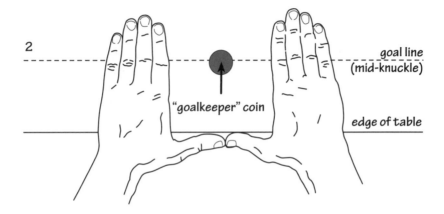

BOWLING

Just take one or more coins and stand them up on their edge. Then either roll or spin coins to knock them over. Scoring can be like the real game, with strikes and spares and even gutter balls.

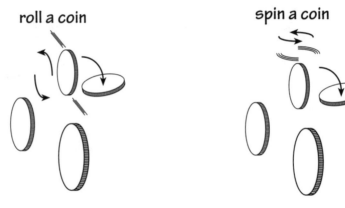

roll a coin

spin a coin

MORE GOOD STUFF TO KNOW

REMEMBERING THE DAYS OF THE MONTHS

Sooner or later we all need to know the number of days in each month. You can teach your child the old rhyme (30 days hath September, April, June, and November, etc.) or just show her this trick.

When you count off the months on your closed hand, the knuckles are the 31-day months and the spaces in between are the 30-day months. That's it. This even catches the two consecutive 31-day months of July and August. Then all your child needs to remember is the 28 (or 29) days in February. Much simpler, isn't it?

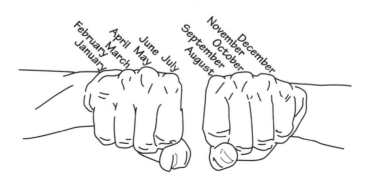

PAPERCLIP EMBRACE

This is another one where a picture is worth 1,000 words. All you need is two paper clips and a piece of paper. Put them all together so that they look like the illustration below. Then hold the two ends of the paper and quickly pull. The two paper clips will snap up into the air and come down linked together!

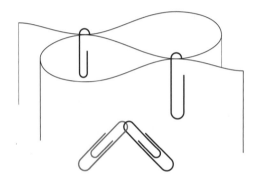

MAKE SPARKS FLY

Don't worry. The sparks here come from nothing more dangerous than Wintergreen Lifesavers™.

If you chew Wintergreen Lifesavers™ in a dark room with your mouth open, you can actually see sparks! So get a pack today!

(What you are seeing is the energy released as the crystals in the candy are broken apart by your chewing. But it looks really good.)

BRUSHING BUBBLES

Here's one for a last bit of fun at bedtime or to induce extra brushing: after brushing your teeth, rinse with carbonated water and watch what happens. (Hint: stay very, very close to the sink.) You can have fun and clean your teeth at the same time.

GUESS SOMEONE'S AGE

Your child can show this magic trick to adults.

Give someone a piece of paper and ask her to write her age. Without looking at the paper, say, "There are 12 months in a year. Add 12 to your age."

Then say, "There are seven days in a week and 52 weeks in a year. Add 752."

Then ask her to tell you the last digit of this number (we'll call this the key number).

Subtract 4 from the key number. (If the key number is smaller than 4, add 10 first and then subtract 4.) The number you end up with will be the last digit of the person's age. Then decide if the person is in her teens, twenties, thirties, etc., and guess to add the right decade.

NEWSPAPER JUNGLE

You can do this for one tree or for a forest. It's simple and you can still recycle the paper when you're done!

Take a section of the newspaper and roll it up tightly. Make four or five cuts about 15–20 cm long at the end without the fold. Now hold the top of the paper where you made the cuts and pull up. The paper will come up in layers with each one having its own leafy branches. The more pages, the leafier your tree will be. A weekend's worth can make a small forest for your child to play with.

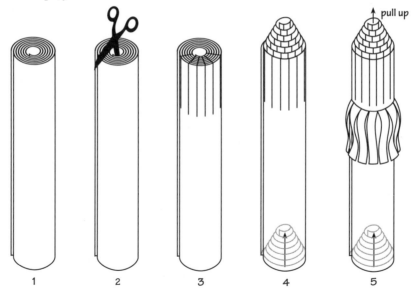

pull up

1   2   3   4   5

CARD TRICKS

There are hundreds of card tricks but I want to give you three of the simplest to start with. They're easy to do, and if you want to share the magic, they're easy to teach so that your child can go out and amaze her friends. (Remember to add some appropriate magic words when performing these.)

This first one is the most basic card trick. The key is to use a deck with a simple, one-way-up design on the backs of the cards. Before you start, make sure the pattern on each card faces the same way.

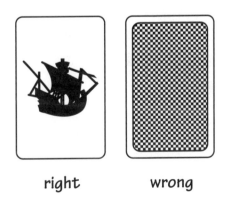

right   wrong

WOW DAD!

 Ask your child to pick a card and memorize it without showing it to you. Shuffle the deck (keeping the pattern facing in one uniform direction). Ask your child to replace the card anywhere in the deck (but have a look to make sure that her pattern points in the opposite direction).

If your child has reversed the card so that the pattern is now going the same way as the deck, you can pull it back for one more shuffle "to make it harder to find" and then turn it as you present it to your child.

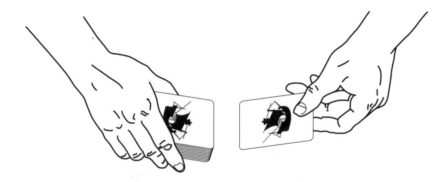

You will know which card was pulled by...um...its aura? Well, you could use that as the magical explanation, but of course it's really the one card in the deck with the design reversed from the others.

For this next one, you again start by asking your child to pick a card and memorize it without showing it to you. Then you cut the deck and ask him to replace his card.

The trick is to look at the card that is showing when you cut the deck. This is called the key card and will be your marker to find your child's card when you sort through the deck.

key card

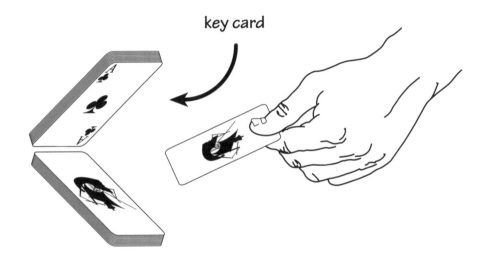

Your child places his card in the cut deck and you put the deck back together with the key card directly on top of your child's card. (You can also carefully cut the deck once or twice to add to the mystery.) Then you sort through the deck, and voila! Your child's card is the one after the key card.

WOW DAD!

This last trick takes a little longer to perform but it also gets your child more involved.

It is also one where a little preparation goes a long way. Start by secretly writing the name of the bottom card of the deck on a piece of paper. If you have the time to prepare this in advance, put the paper somewhere odd, such as inside your shoe, or in your child's lunch box.

Note: Make sure the Jokers have been removed.

Deal 12 cards face down and ask your child to choose any four of them. In this example, we'll say she picks a 3, a King, a 6, and a 9.

Turn these four up and put the other eight face up at the bottom of the deck.

Now deal as many cards as you need face down on top of the four turned-up ones to bring their total to 10. In our example, the 3 needs seven more cards; as in poker, a face card counts as 10 and doesn't need any more; the 4 needs six cards; the 9 needs one. Aces always count as one.

Add the total of the original four cards: $3 + 10 + 6 + 9 = 28$.

Ask your child to choose the 28th card in the deck. Now remove the piece of paper from wherever you hid it and enjoy the oohs and aahs as you show the audience that the card your child chose is the one you wrote down.

A TASTE OF *WOW DAD! 2*

WOW DAD! 2 is also available. It contains another 71 ways to amaze and amuse.

Here are some examples:

LEAF BOAT

You can make this boat just about anywhere to create an instant fleet.

You'll need two leaves (one for the hull of the boat and one for the sail) and a small stick for the mast. Pass the stick through the sail as shown here and stick it into the hull. Launch it on the water and watch it catch the wind.

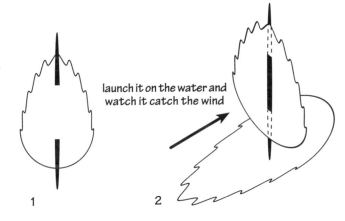

launch it on the water and watch it catch the wind

1

2

DRAWING IN 3-D

Normally this kind of activity requires some training in perspective and other artistically scary things, but there's a trick so that even the least artistic among us can do it.

Just draw a shape twice and connect the opposite points. That's all there is to it.

Cubes are done the same way; they just need a bit of overlapping.

X-RAY VISION

It's not really X-ray vision, of course, but it sure looks as if you can see through your hand.

You start by finding or making a tube: you can use an empty toilet-paper roll or just roll up a piece of paper. Hold the tube up to one eye, and put your other hand next to it.

Open both eyes and you will be able to look through a hole in your hand!

CAN NINE MAKE TEN?

You can do this with nine sticks or toothpicks or straws. Lay them out in front of your audience and ask if they can make nine make ten.

The answer is not a math equation. Just move the nine sticks so that they spell out the letters T E N.

BODY DISTANCES

The distance from your elbow to your wrist is the same as the size of your foot. The length of your outstretched arms is equal to your height.

WOW DAD!

CONTRIBUTE TO THE NEXT *WOW DAD!* BOOK

Do you have a favourite tip or trick that your children love?

Work on the next *WOW DAD!* book is well underway and you can be part of future editions.

Contributors whose submissions are published will be thanked right on the page where their tip appears, along with the name(s) of their children.

To contribute, order the books, or just ask a question, you can reach us…

by WWW: http://www.wowdad.com

by E-Mail: contribute@wowdad.com
orders@wowdad.com
inquiries@wowdad.com

by Phone: 1•877•4WOW DAD Toll Free

by Mail: **Best Guess Publishing**
P.O. Box 238, 1919B – 4 Street SW
Calgary, Alberta T2S 1W4, CANADA

by Fax: **(403) 244•8670**

by Phone: **(403) 244•8688** in Calgary

Don't be shy! Contribute and have another reason to hear *"WOW DAD!"*

Here are some more examples of what's to come to keep you busy.

SAMPLES OF *WOW DAD! 3*

SNOWBALL PYRAMID

This one comes from Sweden. Use enough snowballs to build a pyramid at least four or five rows high. Put a candle in it and you have a truly beautiful winter decoration.

ORANGE PEEL TEETH

This will get them eating fruit. Cut an orange into what my dad used to call 'rockers.' When you're finished eating the fruit stuff, slip the peel inside your mouth for a funny way to smile.

PENNY MAGIC

Find five pennies with a different date on each. Let your audience choose one for you, and then hold it tightly in your closed hand while you explain what you are going to do. Tell your audience that you are going to put all the pennies into a hat (or a bowl or whatever you have) and find the one they chose without looking. (The different dates prove that you have the right penny.)

To find your penny, just pick the warmest one in the hat. A penny is made mostly of copper, so it will hold the heat from your hand for some time even after it's been put in the hat. The keys to this trick are to use only pennies and to make your set-up speech to your audience long enough to give the penny time to get warm. Do this, and you've made magic!

RAINY DAY ART

Rainy days stuck indoors don't have to be miserable. There's lots to do.

Paint a picture with watercolour paints. Then some brave soul can run outside and hang it in the rain in front of the window. As the rain hits it, you can watch a whole new painting being made before your eyes.

Note: For younger children, make sure that they understand what is going to happen to their piece of art before starting this activity. You don't want to be faced with a heartbroken artist.

WOW DAD!

INDEX

All entries in **bold UPPER CASE** indicate principle sections, while **bold Title Case** indicates the activities.

WOW DAD!

ABOUT THE AUTHOR

Peter Atkinson is a dad, but long before that he was a child, born in Ottawa, Canada, in 1961.

After the usual schooling and some unremarkable jobs, he launched a career in the hotel industry, where his first job was setting up tables and chairs in the meeting rooms of the Chateau Laurier Hotel in Ottawa. He eventually worked his way to the hotel front desk, where he was by his own admission the worst cashier on record. But he persevered and ended up holding senior positions with major hotel groups and finally with a hospitality industry consulting firm.

In 1989 Peter married Sandra, who also worked in the hotel business, and their son, Scott, was born three years later. In 1993 work took them all to California. It was there in 1995 that Peter and Sandra divorced, but from here the seeds for *WOW DAD!* were sown out of Peter's "insecurities as a new father and my desire to be a big part of Scott's life."

Although they were no longer married, Peter and Sandra stayed friends and were able to move simultaneously to senior executive positions in England, followed by a move to Singapore in 1997 (Sandra, by this time, had remarried).

Eventually there was talk of another temporary move, this time back to California, but it was decided that it was time for Scott to settle down. Peter was convinced of the importance of fathers playing with their children and how the simplest activities could be the most meaningful and enjoyable. So in December 1998, Peter said goodbye to the corporate world to devote his time to his son, Scott, and to writing *WOW DAD!*

And here we are. Peter and his entire extended family, including Sandra and her new husband, now live very happily in Calgary, Canada.

WOW DAD!

TO ORDER MORE *WOW DAD!*

You can choose one of the following:

1. Order directly at our web site: **http://www.wowdad.com**

2. Phone us toll free: **1•877•4WOW DAD** [that's **1•877•4969•323**] (in Calgary, call **(403) 244•8688**)

3. Send the order form, or a copy of it, by fax to: **(403) 244•8670** or by mail to the following address:

WOW DAD!

P.O. Box 238, 1919B – 4 Street SW

Calgary, Alberta T2S 1W4, CANADA

WOW DAD!

ORDER FORM FOR *WOW DAD!*

PRODUCT View all these products on the web www.wowdad.com	QUANTITY	PRICE EACH		TOTAL
		$US	$CDN	
WOW DAD! Book		$6.95	$8.95	
WOW DAD! 2 Book		$6.95	$8.95	
WOW DAD! *We Have Fun* T-Shirt		$9.95	$14.95	
WOW DAD! Baseball Cap		$7.95	$12.95	
WOW DAD! Multi-Use Pen Knife		$8.95	$13.95	

Send this order form, or a copy of it, by fax to: **(403) 244•8670**

or by mail to: **WOW DAD!**
P.O. Box 238, 1919B – 4 Street SW
Calgary, Alberta T2S 1W4, Canada

SUBTOTAL

SHIPPING & HANDLING

TAX (7% GST in Canada)

TOTAL

METHOD OF PAYMENT

❏ Credit Card

❏ Cheque   ❏ Money Order

Account Number

Expiry   Signature

SHIPPING ADDRESS

Name (of Credit Card Account Holder)

Address

Province/State   Post Code/ZIP

Phone   Fax

SHIPPING & HANDLING RATES

	Books		*Merchandise*	
	First Book	Each Additional Book	First Item	Each Additional Item
Canada	$2.95	$1.50	$2.95	$1.50
USA	$3.95	$2.00	$3.95	$2.00
Overseas	$5.95	$2.50	$8.95	$2.50

WOW DAD!

ORDER SOMETHING FROM *WOW DAD!* FOR A FRIEND

(If you'd like to write a message, or include a greeting card, we'd be pleased to include it with your order.)

PRODUCT View all these products on the web www.wowdad.com	QUANTITY	PRICE EACH $US	$CDN	TOTAL
WOW DAD! Book		$6.95	$8.95	
WOW DAD! 2 Book		$6.95	$8.95	
WOW DAD! *We Have Fun* T-Shirt		$9.95	$14.95	
WOW DAD! Baseball Cap		$7.95	$12.95	
WOW DAD! Multi-Use Pen Knife		$8.95	$13.95	

Send this order form, or a copy of it, by fax to: **(403) 244•8670**

or by mail to: **WOW DAD!**
P.O. Box 238, 1919B – 4 Street SW
Calgary, Alberta T2S 1W4, Canada

SUBTOTAL	
SHIPPING & HANDLING	
TAX (7% GST in Canada)	
TOTAL	

METHOD OF PAYMENT

❏ Credit Card

❏ Cheque   ❏ Money Order

Account Number

Expiry   Signature

Name (of Credit Card Account Holder)

Phone   Fax

ADDRESS FOR GIFT RECIPIENT

Name of Gift Recipient

Address

Province/State   Post Code/ZIP

SHIPPING & HANDLING RATES

	Books		Merchandise	
	First Book	Each Additional Book	First Item	Each Additional Item
Canada	$2.95	$1.50	$2.95	$1.50
USA	$3.95	$2.00	$3.95	$2.00
Overseas	$5.95	$2.50	$8.95	$2.50

WOW DAD!